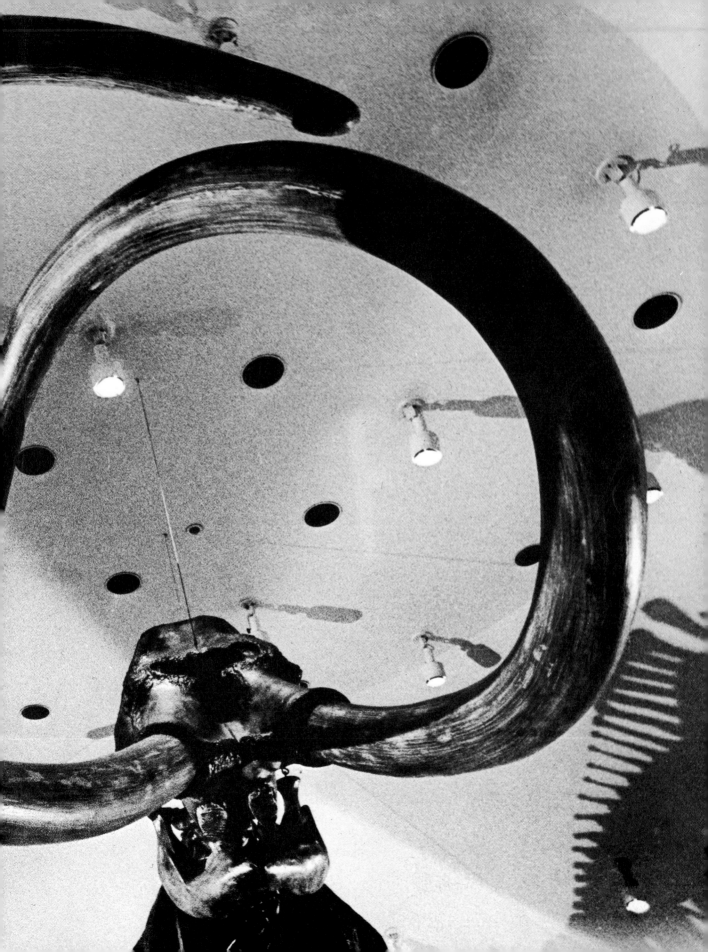

TRAPPED IN·TAR

FOSSILS FROM THE ICE AGE

by
CAROLINE ARNOLD

photographs by
RICHARD HEWETT

CLARION BOOKS

TICKNOR & FIELDS: A HOUGHTON MIFFLIN COMPANY

NEW YORK

The photographs on pages 14 and 21 are from the
Natural History Museum of Los Angeles County.

Clarion Books
Ticknor & Fields, a Houghton Mifflin Company
Text copyright © 1987 by Caroline Arnold
Photographs copyright © 1987 by Richard Hewett

Printed in the U.S.A.

Library of Congress Cataloging-in-Publication Data
Arnold, Caroline.
Trapped in Tar
Includes index.
Summary: Text and photographs examine the work of
scientists studying the fossil remains of prehistoric
animals found in the La Brea tar pits.
1. Vertebrates, Fossil—Juvenile literature. 2. Paleontology—
Pleistocene—Juvenile literature. 3. Paleontology—California
—La Brea Pits—Juvenile literature. [1. Paleontology—Califor-
nia—La Brea Pits.   2. Fossils.   3. La Brea Pits (Calif.)
4. Mammals, Fossil.   5. Prehistoric animals]   I. Hewett,
Richard, ill.   II. Title.
QE841.A74   1987   566'.09794'94   86-17614
ISBN 0-89919-415-X

Y 10 9 8 7 6 5 4 3 2 1

ACKNOWLEDGMENTS

For their cooperation and assistance
in this project we would like to thank
the staff and volunteers of the
George C. Page Museum of La Brea Discoveries,
especially Gregory P. Byrd, superintendent,
George Jefferson, assistant curator,
and Shelly Cox, laboratory supervisor.

We are also grateful to
Linda and Sasha Sircus, Astrid Narins,
Christopher Hewett, and Jennifer and Matthew Arnold
for their cheerful participation
in the photographs.

In the shadow of skyscrapers, a model of an imperial mammoth appears to bellow with rage as it struggles to free itself from the sticky tar below the surface of the water. Like sabertooth cats, giant ground sloths, and many other ancient animals, real mammoths are extinct. Long ago, these animals roamed the grassy plain that is now the busy city of Los Angeles. Then, as now, pools of tar sometimes seeped to the surface of the earth. Water often hid the dangerous tar from view, and thirsty animals came to drink. Little did they know that what looked like a refreshing pool could become their deathtrap.

Large deposits of oil lie under much of southern California. In some places, the oil seeps upward through cracks in the earth's crust. When the oil evaporates, it leaves pools of asphalt, or tar. In cool weather, the tar hardens and the pools become hidden by a layer of leaves and dust. In summer, the hot sun softens the tar into sticky puddles.

A life-size fiberglass model of a female imperial mammoth seems to sink into tar near the George C. Page Museum in Los Angeles, California.

A small animal such as a squirrel or a bird could become stuck when the tar coated its fur or feathers. When a larger animal such as a mammoth waded into the water, its weight made it sink. Its feet became stuck in the tar below and, unable to get out, it eventually died. Then meat-eating animals such as wolves, sabertooth cats, and giant

Bubbles of natural methane gas from deep in the earth constantly rise to the surface of the tar pools.

6

vultures would attack the animal. They too often slipped into the tar and died.

As the flesh of the dead animals rotted away, the bodies floated on the surface of the tar. Later, when the bones became soaked with tar, they sank to the bottom.

The sabertooth cat, shown here in a fiberglass model, was the most feared hunter of the Ice Age.

The deposits of asphalt that trapped these ancient animals are the Rancho La Brea (Bray-a) tar pits. *Brea* is a Spanish word meaning "tar." Once California was part of Mexico and the land around the tar pits was called Rancho La Brea, or ranch of tar. Later, California became a part of the United States and the land belonged to Captain G. Allen Hancock, who operated oil wells there. Today the oil wells are gone, and the land is a county park named after Captain Hancock. In the park are both the tar pits and the George C. Page Museum of La Brea Discoveries.

"Asphalt Is Sticky," an exhibit inside the museum, helps people feel what it might be like to get stuck in tar. Visitors try to lift long steel rods that are immersed in the tar. The tar seems to grab the rods and hold them tight. In the same way, an animal such as a mammoth that stepped into a tar pool found it nearly impossible to escape.

It is difficult to get the steel rod out of the tar even when pulling very hard.

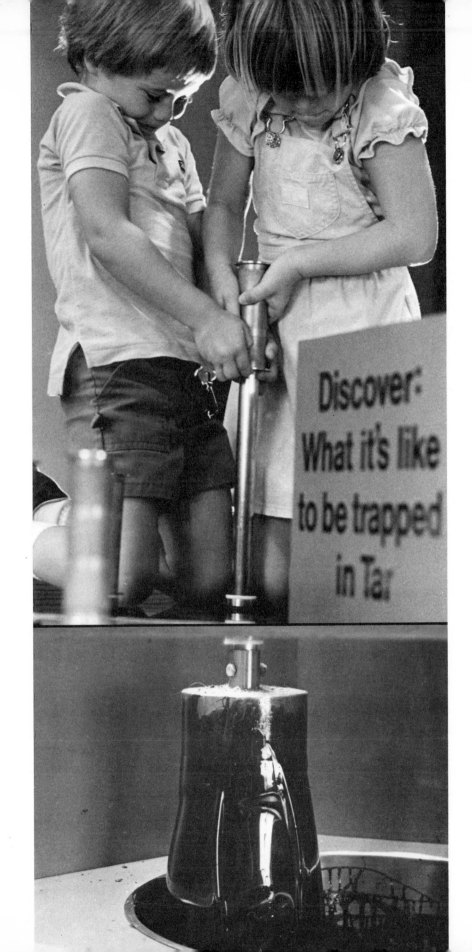

This painting by Jerome and Elma Connolly shows how southern

The bones and plant remains in the Rancho La Brea tar pits are a record of life that existed between 10,000 and 40,000 years ago. Then mammoths, mastodons, sabertooth cats, lions, wolves, sloths, camels, horses, and many other animals lived in North America. The oldest fossil found so far at Rancho La Brea is 38,000 years old. However, most of the fossils are between 14,000 and 16,000 years old.

The fossils in the Rancho La Brea tar pits are from a period of the earth's history known as the Ice Age. Then great sheets of ice, called glaciers, covered much of the Northern Hemisphere. An ice and land bridge connected Asia and North America. Both people and animals migrated across this bridge.

Many different kinds of animals lived near Rancho La Brea. The

California near Rancho La Brea may have looked in the Ice Age.

climate was mild, and food and water were plentiful. When the Ice Age ended about 10,000 years ago, the climate changed. Most of the lakes and streams dried up, and food became scarce. Many of the animals that had once been numerous became extinct.

Today we know about the Ice Age animals because the tar that caused their death also preserved their bones. As the oily tar soaked into the bones, it prevented their decay. Over many years the tar hardened into a solid block composed of tar, dirt, and fossils. Encased in this protective covering, the buried bones were safe for centuries.

Usually we think of fossils as living things that have been turned to stone. However, a fossil is any part of a plant or animal or even the impression of a plant or animal that has been preserved in some way.

For hundreds of years, the native Americans and early European settlers living in California used the tar at Rancho La Brea as a glue for baskets and tools. They also used it to waterproof boats and the roofs of houses. Tar was dug out of the ground at Rancho La Brea and hauled by wagon to wherever it was needed. Although some people noticed bones embedded in the tar, no one paid much attention to them.

Then, in 1906, fossils from Rancho La Brea, which included those of a giant ground sloth, were shown to Dr. John C. Merriam at the University of California. He realized their importance and arranged with Captain Hancock, who owned the land around the tar pits, to remove the bones.

Fossil skeleton of a giant ground sloth.

12

Early excavations were simply holes dug in the ground. The scientists removed the largest bones in the pits and threw away everything else. They took the bones they saved to the Los Angeles County Natural History Museum. There they cleaned them and assembled them into whole skeletons. The skeletons were then displayed in the museum.

Over one hundred pits have been dug in Hancock Park since the early 1900s. Most of them were covered over when the park was landscaped in the 1950s. From the beginning, as each new pit was dug, it was given a number. Currently, you can see six pits. These include the lake pit, which used to be an asphalt quarry, as well as Pit 91, where visitors can watch people dig for fossils.

Right: Blocks of jumbled bones like these were what the first workers discovered.

Facing page: Oil wells dot the background of this early excavation at Rancho La Brea.

Today the excavations are much more careful than the early digs. Each section of the pit is marked, the location of each fossil is precisely noted and recorded, and everything is saved.

To prevent the sides of the pit from collapsing, heavy boards are held against the walls with metal bars. When needed, new boards are added at the bottom. Each year the pit becomes approximately ½-foot deeper. Like most fossil deposits, those at Pit 91 form a large cone shape that becomes narrower as the pit gets deeper. The oldest fossils are found in the lowest layers.

At work in Pit 91.

17

Scientists want to know what is found in the pit as well as where it is found. The bottom of the pit is divided into sections of 3 by 3 feet. When any bone over ½-inch long is revealed, it is measured and photographed in place before it is removed.

Everything that is taken from the pit is placed in large cans. Each can is filled and hauled to the top of the pit. Then it is stored inside the

In each section tar and dirt are chipped away as carefully as possible with trowels, chisels, and dental picks.

museum until the material can be cleaned and sorted. So many fossils have been excavated recently that scientists will need many years to study all of them.

Outdoor excavation at Rancho La Brea is done for only a few months each year. Recently, however, an indoor excavation project was begun that allows people to work year-round.

Water and asphalt continually ooze into the pit bottom. Every day during the excavation, workers must collect this sticky goo in containers.

Between 1906 and 1977, all the material found at the Rancho La Brea tar pits was kept in the Los Angeles County Natural History Museum in Exposition Park. As more and more material was found, it began to overflow the storage rooms at the museum. George C. Page, a Los Angeles businessman, was fascinated with the Rancho La Brea fossils. In 1973, he donated money to build a new museum just for the La Brea discoveries. The museum would also be a center for scientific research.

Thousands of fossils from Rancho La Brea filled the county museum's storage spaces.

In 1975, as bulldozers began to dig the foundation for the new museum, they unearthed a huge deposit of bones. Everyone knew that to excavate these bones at the site would take a long time. This might delay the construction of the museum for years. Instead, they decided to remove the asphalt in large chunks and excavate the bones later. Each portion was cut out, wrapped in a sturdy plaster coating, and stored until the new museum and laboratory were finished. Today visitors can watch through windows as these bone deposits are excavated inside the museum laboratory.

Section of asphalt removed during museum construction. The wire grid helps scientists mark and identify the exact location of each fossil.

Visitors to the museum can watch scientists at work.

People who study the remains of ancient plants and animals are called paleontologists. Much of the work at Rancho La Brea is done by specially trained volunteers. Some of them are students of paleontology; others are people who just want to know more about our ancient heritage. By identifying and studying the bones and plants, paleontologists find they can guess what events might have taken place thousands of years ago.

23

This block of tar and bones contains the skull of a sabertooth cat and parts of the skeletons of two baby horses. Probably the horses became stuck in the tar and then were attacked by the cat. These ancient horses, although similar to present-day horses, became extinct at the end of the Ice Age.

After a bone is removed from the tar and dirt in which it was embedded, it must be cleaned. First, loose dirt is brushed or scrubbed off. Then the bone is soaked and washed in a solvent, a liquid that dissolves the tar. The tar stains the bones brown, so even after cleaning, the bones remain dark. The clean bones are then labeled and set aside for identification and cataloguing.

The teeth and eye sockets are visible in the sabertooth cat skull (right).
Lying next to it are the horse leg bones (center).

Fossil bones are often found broken into many small pieces.

Sometimes bones are broken, or pieces of skeletons are scattered over a wide area. Putting them back together is a bit like assembling a jigsaw puzzle. Here the pieces of a mammoth hipbone are being put back together. After the bones have been sorted, they are placed in large storage trays.

26

Whole skeletons are rarely found in the tar deposits. Usually they broke up on the surface of the tar. Then, as a skeleton sank to the bottom of a shallow tar seep, new tar bubbling up from below would move the bones about. As more bones gathered at the bottom of the pool, they were all jumbled together. The skeletons on display in the George C. Page Museum contain bones from many different animals.

Bones are catalogued before they are stored. Scientists use the large collection of Rancho La Brea fossils for a variety of studies.

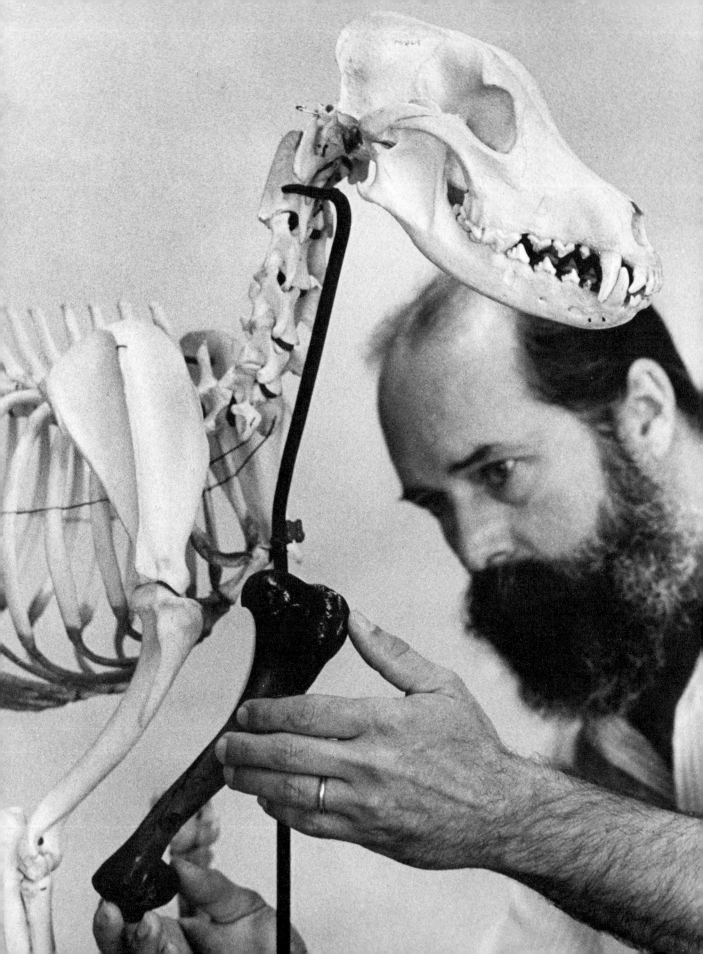

Facing page: A whole skeleton of a modern dog is useful for comparison with fossil bones of ancient wolves. Above: Sorting back bones of dire wolves.

Most fossils found at Rancho La Brea are used for scientific research. Scientists from all over the world study the La Brea fossils. Bones are often sent to other museums. Sometimes, instead of sending a bone, a plaster cast is made of it.

The remains of over 420 different kinds of animals are among the Rancho La Brea discoveries. Experts are able to identify what kind of animal a bone belonged to by looking at its size and shape and by comparing it with other fossils. To figure out how the bones might be put together in a skeleton, they may compare them with similar bones in a modern animal.

This fossil skeleton is composed of bones from imperial mammoths, the biggest animals found at Rancho La Brea. These majestic beasts, with their huge ivory tusks, once roamed throughout the southern half of North America. An adult mammoth could be over 13

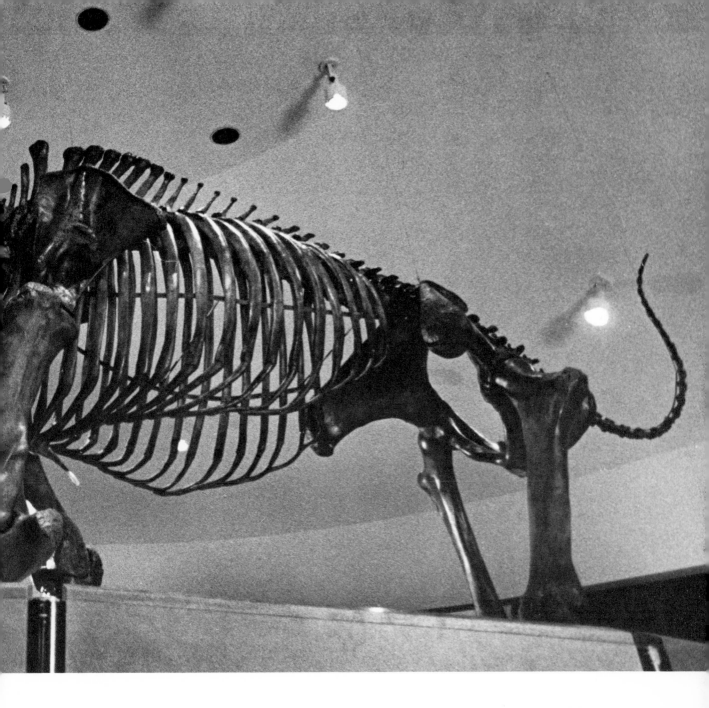

feet (3.9 meters) tall, and could weigh about 10,000 pounds (4,900 kilograms). A smaller mammoth lived in Europe and Asia during the Ice
Age and is depicted in ancient cave paintings found in France. It had
a shaggy fur coat to keep it warm in cold weather. It too is extinct.

The mammoths are closely related to the slightly smaller modern elephants. Like the elephants, mammoths fed on grass and leaves, and for this they had four large, flat teeth. A single mammoth molar could be a foot long! As the molars became worn by chewing, they moved forward in the mouth and were replaced by a new set. A mammoth could have six sets of teeth during its lifetime. After its sixth set was worn out, it would die of starvation.

Bones of a more distant relative of the elephant, the American mastodon, are also found at Rancho La Brea. The mastodon was smaller than a mammoth or elephant, being only about 6 feet (1.8 meters) tall.

The large flat tooth of a mammoth (left) was good for chewing. The jagged teeth in the mastodon jaw (right) were better for eating twigs and leaves.

Ground sloths were another group of large Ice Age mammals, now extinct, whose bones are found at Rancho La Brea. The largest, Harlan's ground sloth, weighed about 3,500 pounds (1,600 kilograms). An unusual feature of its skeleton is a series of pea-size knobs at the back of the neck. These knobs may have been a kind of armor protecting it from an attack by an animal such as a sabertooth cat. Two other types of ground sloths found at Rancho La Brea were smaller and did not have these bony knobs. Like their closest modern-day relatives, the tree sloths of Central and South America, the ancient ground sloths were slow-moving plant eaters.

Like the ancient ground sloths, these life-size cement models located outside the museum are over 6 feet (1.8 meters) high.

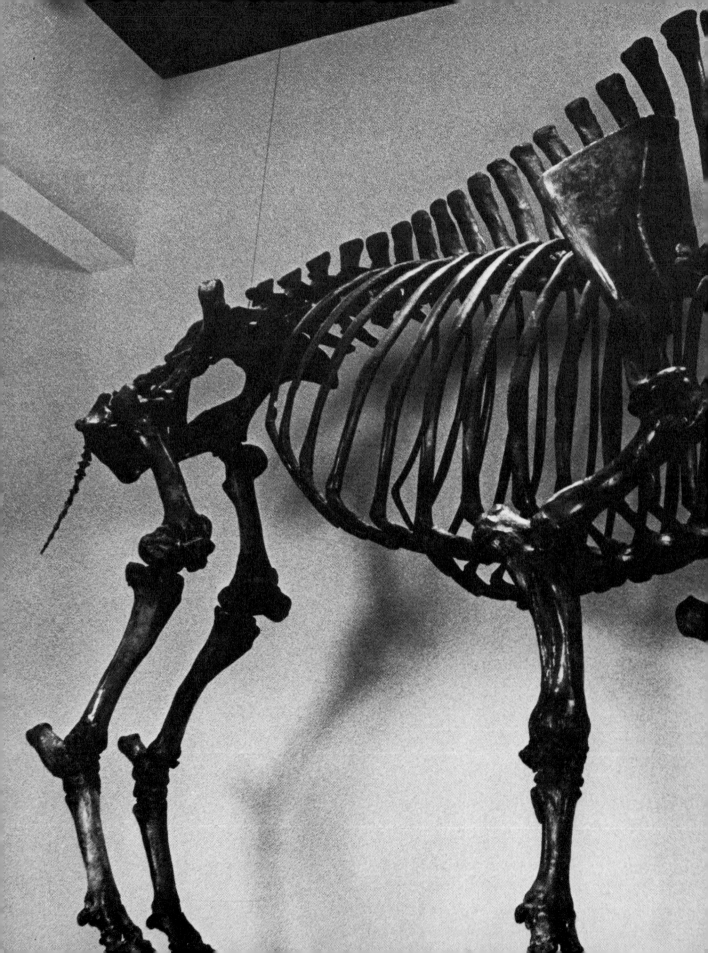

Plant eaters, like the sloths and this ancient bison, are called herbivores. Other large herbivores that roamed the ancient plain included horses, camels, and deer. All of these, as well as smaller animals such as tapirs, peccaries, rabbits, mice, and squirrels, were potential victims of the meat eaters.

A weekly dusting keeps this bison skeleton clean.

Meat eaters are called carnivores. The majority of bones found at Rancho La Brea are from carnivores. Some carnivores hunt other animals and kill them. Others are scavengers and only eat animals they find that are already dead.

Members of the dog family form the largest group of fossils found at Rancho La Brea. They include bones of the dire wolf, coyote, grey fox, and two types of domestic dogs.

The remains of more than 1,600 dire wolves—more than those of any other single animal—have been found at Rancho La Brea. The dire wolf lived throughout North America during the Ice Age. Usually dire wolves hunted in packs, chasing their prey across the plain until it tired and then attacking and killing it. Sometimes the pack attacked an animal trapped in tar. Unfortunately, many wolves became victims of the tar as well.

Dire wolf skeleton. The dire wolf looked very much like the present-day grey wolf. Its strong jaws and large teeth were good for crushing bones.

One of the most fearsome hunters of the Ice Age was the sabertooth cat, with its strong jaws and sharp canine teeth. Like the dire wolf, it could be tempted by an easy meal of an animal trapped in the tar, only to become trapped itself.

The sabertooth cat was about the size of a modern-day lion. It could run fast in short bursts of speed. However, it probably caught its prey by slowly sneaking up on it, and then, when it was close enough, using its strong legs to pounce for the kill. Some paleontologists think that sabertooths may have lived and hunted in small packs.

Left: Bones of over one thousand sabertooth cats have been found at Rancho La Brea. The sabertooth cat is the California state fossil.

Facing page: Sabertooth cat skull. The two large upper teeth, called sabers, could grow to be 8 inches (20 centimeters) long.

Unlike any of the modern cats, the sabertooth had two huge, knifelike teeth in its upper jaw. No one knows exactly how the sabertooth used these teeth. However, some scientists now think that the sabertooth used them to rip open the soft underbelly of its victim.

A predator perhaps even more deadly than the sabertooth cat was the American lion. Like the slightly smaller modern African lion, the American lion was strong, agile, and a superb hunter. Probably it

Although the sabertooth cat is sometimes called a sabertooth tiger, sabertooth cat is the preferred name.

The American lion (left) was taller and heavier than the sabertooth cat (right).

hunted alone or in pairs. It is extinct now, but during the Ice Age it roamed throughout North America.

Not as many lions met their death in the tar pits as did the sabertooths. Perhaps there were fewer of them or perhaps they did not commonly live in the Rancho La Brea area. Other members of the cat family whose bones have been found at Rancho La Brea are the bobcat, the jaguar, and two species of the puma.

The largest carnivore found at Rancho La Brea is the short-faced bear. Unlike modern bears, it had unusually long legs that were good for chasing prey. Like modern bears, the short-faced bear probably ate both plants and animals. By studying the shape of its teeth, scientists are trying to find out whether meat or plants formed the main part of its diet. The short-faced bear is now extinct. The bones of two living species, the black bear and the grizzly bear, have also been found in the tar pits.

The smallest carnivores found in the tar pits are weasels, skunks, badgers, ring-tailed cats, and raccoons. The most common of these is the weasel. It probably came to the tar pits to catch animals such as rats and mice that had become trapped there.

Facing page: Life-size cement model of the short-faced bear.
Below: Short-faced bear skull.

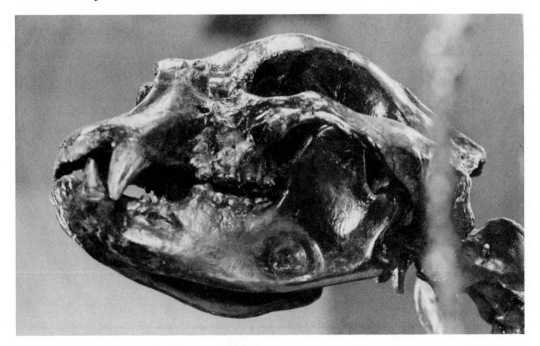

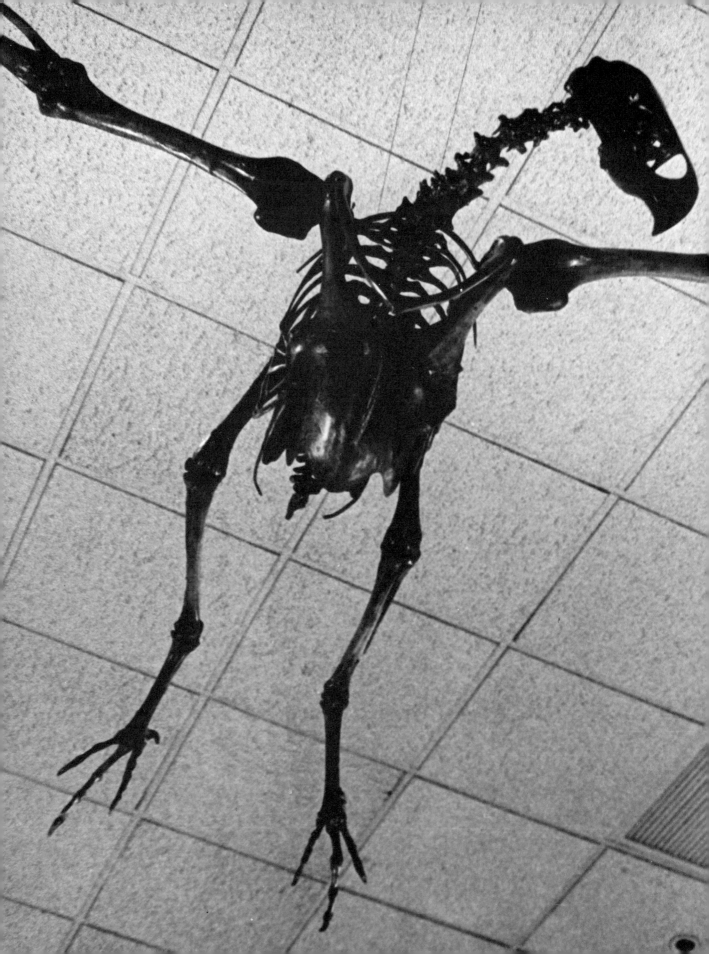

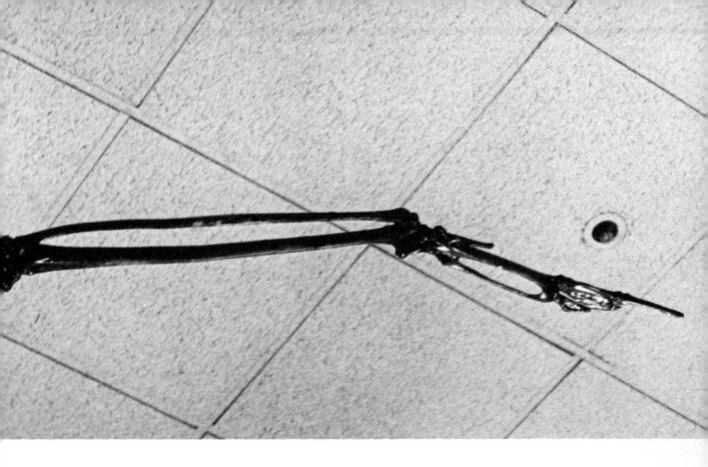

Over 135 different species of birds have been identified from bones in the tar pits. Many of these birds were meat eaters, which, like other predators, may have been attracted to animals struggling in the tar. Some of these birds include nine different kinds of owls and more than twenty different kinds of hawks, eagles, and falcons.

Ancestors of the living California condor are among the victims of the tar. Although the condor is very big, it is not as big as the largest bird discovered at Rancho La Brea, Merriam's teratorn. Fossil bones of over one hundred teratorns have been found in the tar pits. This now-extinct relative of the modern stork had a wingspan of nearly 14 feet (3.2 meters), weighed about 30 pounds (13–14 kilograms), and was about 30 inches (77 centimeters) tall. It is thought that the teratorn walked on its long legs, stalking its prey on the ground. Then, after catching the animal, the teratorn swallowed it whole.

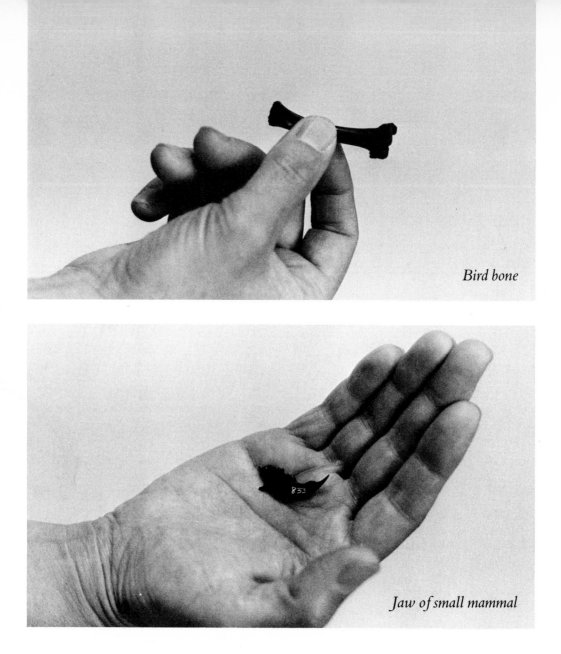

Bird bone

Jaw of small mammal

In addition to many kinds of mammals and birds, the remains of over three hundred other kinds of animals have been found at Rancho La Brea. They include lizards, snakes, turtles, toads, frogs, and fish, as well as clams, snails, and many insects and spiders. Many of these animals still live today in California. Animals such as freshwater clams that no longer live at Rancho La Brea provide evidence that in the Ice Age,

48

Pine cone

Snail shells

there were ponds and streams at Rancho La Brea during at least part of the year.

Fossil plants found at Rancho La Brea also provide clues to the landscape in ancient times. So far, over 100,000 plant fossils have been found in the tar pits. They vary from pieces of wood, leaves, cones, and seeds to tiny microscopic remains.

The most impressive finds in the Rancho La Brea tar pits are the huge bones of long-extinct animals such as the mammoths and the sabertooth cats. However, some of the most interesting new information about the Ice Age is revealed in fossils almost too tiny to see. These very small fossils, called microfossils, are embedded in the tar next to the larger bones.

In this exhibit at the George C. Page Museum visitors can feel the fossilized leg bone of a giant ground sloth.

The tar is removed from the microfossils by placing them on a wire screen, which is then immersed into boiling solvent. After the tar dissolves, the remaining material is removed and dried. It is a mixture of sand, small pebbles, and very small fossils. The fossils include seeds and small plant remains, snails, insect parts, and bones and teeth of small animals. These are separated under a magnifying glass and then identified and catalogued.

Seeds and pollen of ancient plants help scientists to know what the climate was like at Rancho La Brea long ago.

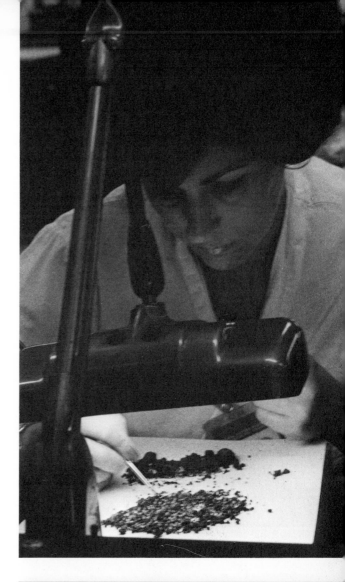

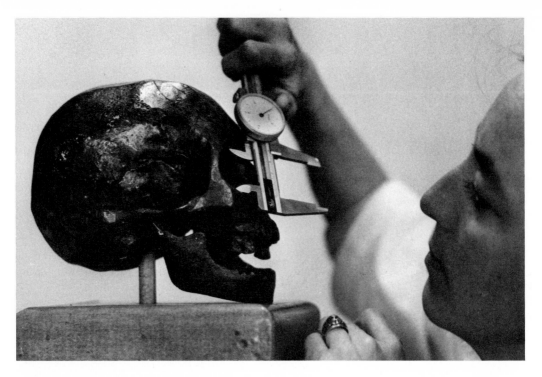

Measurements of this ancient skull of a female human help scientists estimate what her body size might have been.

Ancient humans may have arrived in North America as early as 30,000 years ago. Yet, in contrast to the huge number of animal bones taken from the Rancho La Brea tar pits, the bones of only one human have ever been found there. The bones are about 9,000 years old.

In 1914, the skull and partial skeleton of a twenty- to twenty-five-year-old woman was discovered in one of the pits. She was about 4 feet 10 inches (1.5 meters) tall, and her teeth suggest that she lived on a diet of stone-ground meal. Although marks on her skull show that she was hit in the head, no one knows for certain how she died or how she got into the tar pit. She may have been murdered and thrown into the tar, or she may have been buried and then had tar seep into her grave.

Recently, when the foundation for a large office building was being dug, a new group of fossils was revealed.

One idea as to why the large animals of the Ice Age became extinct about 10,000 years ago is that they were overhunted by early humans. Although hunters may have hastened their extinction, many scientists believe that severe changes in the climate were more important. As the ice receded and temperatures became warmer, many of the lakes and streams in the western United States dried up. With the change in climate, different kinds of plants began to grow. Some animals could not adapt to the new weather and food supply.

Throughout the Hancock Park area of Los Angeles, there are tar seeps, many filled with bones. Occasionally people discover them when digging in their gardens.

Asphalt deposits similar to those at Rancho La Brea have been found in other parts of California, as well as in Iran, Peru, Russia, and Poland. However, none has such a rich collection of ancient plant and animal remains.

The Rancho La Brea discoveries provide a unique opportunity to study in detail what life was like in the Ice Age. Because there are so many fossils at Rancho La Brea, scientists can learn how an animal grew and developed and, in some cases, even what it ate or what kinds of diseases it might have had.

By finding out more about plants and animals that lived in North America between 10,000 and 40,000 years ago, we can begin to understand the kinds of problems early humans faced as they arrived here. Learning how the earth changed in the past, and how some animals survived and others could not, may help us to prepare for the future.

Realistic three-quarter-size model of a mastodon.

INDEX

Page numbers in *italics* refer to captions

American lions, 42-43, *43*
Asphalt. *See* Tar

Bears, 45, *45*
  short-faced, 45, *45*
Bison, 37, *37*

Carnivores, 39-45
  small, found at La Brea, 45
Cat family, 43. *See also* Sabertooth
  cats
Cave paintings, 31
Condor, California, 47

Dog family, *29*, 39. *See also* Wolves

Elephants, 32
Excavating for fossils, 12, 15, *15*
  delayed excavations, 22
  modern methods, 17-19, *18*
  photography, use of, 18
  Pit 91, 15, *17*
Extinction of Ice Age large animals,
  53

Fossils, 10, 11, 20
  American lions, 42-43, *43*
  bears, 45, *45*
  bison, 37, *37*
  carnivorous birds, 47, *47*
  cleaning of, 25, 51
  dire wolves, *29*, 39, *39*
  discovered when excavating for
    new building, *53*
  excavation of, 12, 15-19, *15*, *17*
  frequently broken or scattered, 26
  ground sloths, *12*, 35, *50*
  human, 52
  imperial mammoths, 30-31
  from La Brea, research uses for,
    29
  Merriam's teratorns, 47
  microfossils, 50-51, *51*
  other, 48-49
  plant, 49, *49*
  sabertooth cats, *40*, *43*
  small carnivores, 45

George C. Page Museum of La Brea
  Discoveries, *5*, 8, 20

56

delayed excavation of fossils for, 22, *23*
sloth's leg bone at, *50*

Hancock, Capt. G. Allen, 8, 12
Park, 8, 15, 53
Herbivores, 37
Horses, ancient, 10, 25, 37

Ice Age, *7*, 10, 11, *11*, 25, 31, 35, 39, 40, 43, 48, 50
extinction of large animals from, 53
Los Angeles, California, 5, *5*
Los Angeles County Natural History Museum, 15, 20

Mammoths, 5, *5*, 6, 8, 10, 31–32
imperial, 5, *5*, 30–31
teeth, 32, *32*
Mastodons, 32, *54*
teeth, 32, *32*
Merriam, Dr. John C., 12
Methane gas, *6*

Oil, 5, 8, *15*

Page, George C., 20. *See also* George C. Page Museum
Paleontologists, 23, 40
Pit 91, 15, 17–18, *17*

Rancho La Brea tar pits, 8, 10, 12
appearance in Ice Age, *10–11*, 48–49
best source for plant and animal research, 54

breakup of skeletons in, 27
excavation of fossils, 12, 15–19, *15*, *17*
fossils found in, 10, 12, *15*, 30, 32
microfossils from, 50–51, *51*
museum for fossils from, *5*, 8, 20, 22, *23*, *50*
only human fossil find, 52, *52*
variety of animals found, 6–7, 10–11, 27, 30–49

Sabertooth cats, 5, 6, *7*, 10, 25, *25*, 40–43, *40*, *41*, *42*, *43*
teeth, 40, *40*, 42
Scavengers, 39
Sloths, ground, 5, 10, 12, *12*
fossils found at La Brea, 12, 35, *50*
size of, 35, *35*

Tar, 5, *5*
getting stuck in, 6–7
how formed, 5
preservation of bones in, 7–10, 11
removed during museum construction, 22, *22*
removing from excavation pits, *19*
removing from fossils, *18*, 25
seeps and deposits elsewhere, 53–54
stickiness of, 8, *8*
uses for, 12
Teratorns, Merriam's, 47

Water
oozing into excavation pits, *19*
tar hidden by, 5
Wolves, 6, 10, 39
dire, *29*, 39, *39*

CAPISTRANO UNIFIED SCHOOL DISTRICT
32972 CALLE PERFECTO
SAN JUAN CAPISTRANO, CA. 92675